BROKEN GRATITUDE

SAMMY FARRENS

Inquiries and Book Orders should be addressed to:

 Great Writers Media

Great Writers Media
Email: info@greatwritersmedia.com
Phone: 877-600-5469

ISBN: 978-1-960939-88-3 (sc)
ISBN: 978-1-960939-92-0 (hc)
ISBN: 978-1-960939-89-0 (ebk)

FOREWORD

At 16 years old, I landed my first sales job at Circuit City, and it was a base plus commission gig. Despite being the youngest salesman, I was eager and excited to work alongside the other salesmen, who were much older and experienced. While it was just a part-time job for me, a means to an end before college or a more fulfilling career, for them, it was a career.

One day, a man with paint all over his hands and overalls walked into the store. While the other salesmen dismissed him as someone who wasn't serious about buying anything, I saw him as a potential customer. To my surprise, he was there to buy a new big-screen TV, a state-of-the-art surround sound system, and everything in between. I don't remember how much I made on that sale, but it was enough to make the older salesmen envious. That experience taught me an invaluable lesson: not to judge a book by its cover.

Fast forward 25 years later, another man with paint on his hands asked me to be on his podcast Mental Edge. Sammy Farrens is someone who primarily works in the trades, while I have spent most of my career in white-collar work. Initially, we seemed to have nothing in common, but after talking to Sammy, I was blown away by his depth of knowledge and insight on mental toughness, forgiveness, and letting go. I watched him interact with men and women from all walks of life at a leadership retreat I hosted, and his trials, tribulations, and life experiences have enabled him to provide thoughtful advice.

In a world full of smoke and mirrors, fake social media influencers, and authors who write books on clout instead of real-life wisdom, Sammy Farrens is one of the most genuine people I know. In this book, Sammy shares five positive and powerful lessons he was taught by his courageous mother, which he calls 5 for 5. As you read through Sammy's real and raw emotional stories and commit to learning and living these lessons, I believe your life will be transformed in a meaningful way. Take the journey, enjoy the ride, and find the gratitude inside you.

ACKNOWLEDGMENTS

Writing a book was something that had never crossed my mind until I started posting on TikTok. Through the support of my followers, I found the inspiration and motivation to give it a try. Initially, I thought writing a book would be easy – just put some words on paper and hope for the best. However, I quickly realized that I would need a lot of help along the way.

I am immensely grateful to Seth Clint, a consultant at Great Writers Media, who guided me through the entire process. When we first spoke, I didn't even know what a manuscript was, let alone what it takes to write a book. Thanks to his expertise, my thoughts and experiences have been transformed into the book you are about to read.

I would also like to express my heartfelt appreciation to Pastor Jim Blue of Sunrise Church in Ofallon, Mo. His knowledge of scriptures and his personal talks on gratitude and Jesus Christ helped me find peace during moments when I felt overwhelmed with writing.

In life, we encounter people who radiate integrity and goodness. Josh Kosnick is one such person, and I knew from the moment I met him that he was the perfect choice to write the foreword for this book. Thank you, Josh, for continuing to inspire those around you with your amazing personality.

I must also extend my gratitude to my wife, Janet, who sacrificed her time to be with me and kept me accountable throughout this journey. This book would not have been possible without you.

To my mom, I owe my life, love, and gratitude. As you will read, she is the biggest reason why I live a life of gratitude.

Lastly, I want to thank myself and my commitment to living a life of gratitude. It has been an ongoing journey, and writing this book has allowed me to reflect on the people and experiences that have shaped my perspective.

INTRODUCTION

My Gratitude

*"Start children off on the way they should go,
and even when they are old they will not turn from it."*
Proverbs 22:6

A few years ago, a gentleman asked me who was my mentor. So many names went through my head (Tony Robbins, Les Brown, Andy Frisella, Ed Mylett, John Maxwell, etc.). However, only one name stuck out and I knew that it was the only answer I could give, MOM!

My mentor never walked, never ran, never rode a bike, nor did so many things we take for granted every day. My mentor wasn't rich, didn't drive a fancy car, and definitely didn't have a big exotic house. My mentor/My mom lived her life in a wheelchair. She lived her life with a full metal brace on her right leg and a shoe that was three sizes too big because her right foot was that much smaller than her left foot. The brace was for the times that someone would help her up to stand because her leg wasn't strong enough to hold her. Walking might consist of three to four steps at the most then it was time to sit back down because that's all her leg could handle at the time. The only time the brace came off was bedtime. My mom had polio throughout her body, and while it mainly affected one of her legs, her arms, later in life it spread to her spine.

Polio is a viral infection causing nerve injury which leads to partial or full paralysis in parts of the body. Polio vaccines were introduced in the 1950's and still are used today. Polio now affects less than 1% of the world's population.

We were a poor to a medium-class family, living in a small town in mid-Missouri where jobs were not that plentiful, especially for a woman in a wheelchair. But that didn't hold my mom back from providing the best life she could for me and my sister Amber. She had envelopes for different holidays (Christmas, birthdays, Easter, etc.), and no matter what, every week she would put a little bit of money in each envelope so that we would at least get something for each holiday. I think that she learned the envelope trick from Dave Ramsey or from some other book she read.

In life, we all have certain things that hold us back, whether it's our physical abilities or mindset. Mom knew that her physical abilities were not going to change so she turned to her mindset. She read books all the time. Mostly Stephen Kings and romance books, but she would throw an educational or motivational book in, from time to time.

When she wasn't reading, she would write poetry, poems of love, sadness, heartache, joy, and forgiveness. I have a whole box full of poems she wrote throughout her life. Most of them were to Jesus. There are quite a few for Grandpa Vaughn, who passed in 1993. She wrote poems about everyone, me and my sister, our cousins, Grandma Vaughn, and pretty much anyone she knew. Now, reading her poems, I can feel the emotions she poured into every word.

She also prayed, A LOT. I didn't realize how strong her faith was until later in my life. Looking back, I think that prayer is where she got her strength for life, love, and happiness from.

While I'm sure mom went through a lot of physical and mental hardships because of the polio, I can't and won't tell you I know what she was thinking all the time. But I can and will tell you, her actions were that of *Gratitude*. She showed gratitude to everyone she came in contact with, and for that I believe she lived a full life. From that wheelchair, she babysat 22 kids for five or six years, she worked at a shoe factory for 16 years, and her life ended working with special needs adults. Through all these ventures, I'm sure she always wanted to make more money, but her driving force was being kind to others and knowing God would provide. Her lesson for everyone was to be grateful for even the littlest of things you have.

The five main lessons she taught me will be covered throughout this book. Five lessons that if followed you will feel and receive more gratitude, happiness, and love than you might have known existed. I call these lessons the five for five.

Five Positive And Powerful Changes To Start Making In Your Life

1. **Evaluate Your Environment.**
   Who do you surround yourself with? Where is your energy at?

2. **No More Negative Self-Talk.**
   What you say and think become your beliefs. What you believe is where your actions will take you. Your actions are the final factors in who you truly are in life.

3. **Let Go of What You Cannot Control.**
   Understand and accept that you don't control everything inside yourself and you barely control anything going on outside of yourself.

4. **Stay Away from Other People's Drama and Negativity.**
   What situations do you find yourself in? What are your boundaries and limits? Who is in your inner circle?

5. **Be Honest with Yourself about Yourself.**
   Reflect on the decisions in your past, figure out your purpose, most of all, develop your mental toughness and self-awareness.

These are five not so easy things to do. Five things that will take daily practice and consistency. Five things that once you have accomplished them will bring you a life of Gratitude.

While mom was teaching me these five lessons my whole life, I didn't truly understand them until June 27th 2008. That would be the last day I would ever speak face to face with her.

I got a phone call from my sister Amber early that evening saying that mom was being taken to Mexico, Missouri to the hospital, but she didn't know all the details. As fast as I could I got in the car and headed to Mexico, which was about a 45-minute drive. All I could think of was what could it be this time? Mom had been getting worse over the last few months with the polio advancing causing the doctors to want to fuse the vertebra in her neck. Then they found hepatitis A in her blood which they figured was from a blood transfusion she had in her twenties. And now, cancer which was shutting down her whole body.

Upon arriving at the hospital, I ran into the ER trying to locate mom. I was asking everyone where she was but no one seemed to know. I felt like no one cared and I was just bothering everyone. I tried so hard to keep my cool because I knew that getting angry wasn't going to help, so I just kept asking. Finally, in a panic, I screamed at one of the nurses to please help me find her. Then I fell to the floor and started crying. I just wanted to see my mom.

The nurse that I screamed at apologized and we figured out that she was in a transport to Columbia, Missouri to the University Hospital. The nurse let me know that the Mexico hospital wasn't set up for the care that mom needed.

So back in the car I went, now headed to Columbia. On the way, it hit me that I didn't see Amber nor my stepdad Bob. I just figured they were on their way to Columbia also. It also hit me that I never asked what was going on with mom. So, for the next twenty-five minutes, I had to wonder about that. What a night and little did I know, it wasn't even started.

Now located at Columbia University Hospital ER I was again stuck with no answers. The person at the help desk didn't have any idea who I was talking about when I was telling him my mom's name.

He also had no idea of her being transported from Mexico to them. I was at the breaking point with the help desk guy who was no damn help at all, so I started looking for Amber and Bob.

Not able to find them I sat down to settle down. I could feel my heartbeat in my hands, I felt like I couldn't take a deep breath, and my head was starting to hurt. Through all of the chaos, I started thinking about Bob and what would happen to him when mom was gone.

I will never forget the first time I met Bob. He and mom met on the internet in a chat room and had been talking for a few months when he decided to come to see her from Arkansas. The day he arrived I had to work but I made sure a bunch of people were with mom at her house. When I got off work, I rushed over to meet the internet fella that wanted to date my mom. I walked into mom's house to see eight to ten people all gathered around the kitchen table. Uncles, cousins, Amber, Mom in her regular spot, and Bob to the left of her holding her hand.

The kitchen went crazy quiet as I walked towards the table. Bob stood up, took a couple of steps toward me, and extended his hand to introduce himself. I remember being calm at that moment but at the same time intrigued. I didn't raise my hand, I simply said "You and I need to talk outside, NOW." Then I hear mom "Sammy what are you doing? Keep your cool." Bob said to mom, "It's okay, we just need to talk."

Once outside as we stood face to face, I told Bob the one rule I had for dating my mother. I said, "That woman at that table is my life and my world, if you ever hurt her physically or mentally, you will die. A slow painful fucking death, do you understand the rule?" Bob replied, "Yes sir I do, now that I know the rules, can I shake your hand?" I knew then that Bob would be good for mom. Bob said that story at their wedding, and swore: "For the rest of my life, I will never break the rule."

After about ten minutes of sitting in the waiting room, I see mom being wheeled into the ER in a bed sitting up. Finally, I could calm down and get some answers. My first question to mom was where Amber and Bob were. She told me she sent them home because there was nothing to worry about and she would be okay. She told them to just come to check on her tomorrow. Then she told me to head back home also and that she would be okay. She just wasn't feeling right but she would be fine.

Well, that didn't work for me so I proceeded in telling her I would stay the night and it wasn't up for discussion. Not that I wanted to press my luck but every once in a while, I could talk back to her without getting popped in the mouth.

Once in her room and she had a drink and enough blankets to make the devil hot we sat and talked, laughed, cried, and I held her hand all night.

We talked about finding a purpose in life and going after it with all I had. I didn't quite understand what a purpose was much less my own purpose. She explained that to her a purpose is something that you love. Something that you look forward to every day, even on the bad days. A purpose that makes you want to live for tomorrow and wish that today would never end.

She told me that it's okay to cut people out of your life and still love them. Family and friends included. She explained that as each one of us goes on our different paths in life we will have to love those people from a distance. It's not a negative thing, it's the fact that as you go higher in life, some people don't and won't want to go with you. You will lose relationships along the way; you may go right while they are going left. Sometimes, you just have to wave and wish them well on their journey.

We had a long discussion on being honest with yourself and loving yourself FIRST. I told her I would always love my kids first because that's the way she raised me. I didn't know what to think when she told me that I and my sister have always been her third most loved thing on the planet. First was God, then herself, then us kids. She explained it to me like this. If she had a glass of water and I wanted a drink she would only be able to give me as much water as she had put into the glass. The more water she filled up her glass the more water she could give me. That's the way love works, we can only give as much as we have in ourselves. While you might think you are giving your loved ones everything you have, you need to check your own glass and see how full it really is.

That's the honesty part.

She told me a story of when she was a little kid and her brothers were all riding their bikes (she had three brothers). She remembered being so mad at them because they got to do something she couldn't do. She said even as a little kid she was mad because God had made her this way and it wasn't fair. She said the boys were teasing her saying that she should race them because they only had two tires and her wheelchair had four. The madder she got the more they teased.

What mom and the brothers didn't know was that grandma was listening to this the whole time. Mom said grandma came out on the porch and told them boys to put their bikes away and they didn't get to ride them anymore that day. Then she grabbed mom's wheelchair and told mom that they were going to get ice cream.

The boys of course threw a fit and said they were sorry and wouldn't do it again, but grandma said, "Nope, you all made your bed, now lay in it."

Mom explained to me that day changed her life. She learned that she couldn't control everything, how being around negative people never turned out good, and that God had a plan for her whether she could see it or not. Mom said that day she was thankful to be in that wheelchair because she got ice cream and them mean boys didn't.

Mom was simple like that; it wasn't always about the big things in life but more about enjoying the little things.

I wish that night would have lasted forever, but unfortunately, morning came and the nurses and doctors started making their rounds. Around 7:00 a.m., they drew some blood and said they needed to run some tests. Mom fell asleep not long after the nurse left the room and I sat there just holding her hand. Around 8:30 a.m., mom's doctor came into the room and asked if he could see me in the hallway.

Spending the whole night with mom, I didn't even realize that no one had given us any updates or told me what was really going on. So now, standing in the hallway my heart was racing and my brain had a million thoughts going through it.

While I don't remember the doctor's name, I will never forget what he said, "I'm very sorry to tell you this but you should start calling all of your mom's family and friends because her organs are slowly shutting down and she probably only has a couple of days left."

I knew walking back into that room I had to be strong so I held back the tears and put on a fake smile. Back at mom's side I grabbed her hand again and started to talk about anything else except what I had just heard. Mom knew though, as moms always do.

She asked me what the doctor had said, and as I started to lie, she cut me off and simply said, "I'm going to die in here, aren't I?"

I couldn't say anything, it was like my mouth was glued shut. My brain kept telling me to look away and lie to her. Tell her anything but the truth because if I say it out loud it will make it true and I'm not ready for her to be gone. Not being able to say anything, I just shook my head yes.

I hugged her as we cried and I never wanted to let her go. After what seemed like forever, I sat back down as mom started to talk. She said to me that there was a reason I got to stay the night with her and be there with her in the morning when the doctor came with the news.

She told me that everyone would be showing up soon and I had a job to do and I was the only one strong enough to do it. Around 10:30 a.m., I was standing in the waiting room with all of our family and a bunch of friends. A few minutes before, I had told everyone that I needed them in the waiting room to give them an update. As I stood there ready to speak, all I could focus on was grandma. It was a time when I told a mother she was losing a daughter, a daughter she was losing a mom, a husband he was losing a wife, and a family they were losing the glue that held us all together.

On July 2nd, 2008 around 10:30 p.m., I stood by mom's bed holding her hand. I was looking at all the machines that were keeping her alive, willing for a miracle to happen, and hoping she would wake up. The doctors had put her in a coma so she wouldn't be in so much pain as her organs shut down. She hadn't spoken since way early that morning before I got to the hospital. I remember asking the doctor if he could wake her up for just a minute so I could say goodbye and that I loved her. He told me that would be so painful for her that there was no way he would do it. Frustrated but understanding I looked back at mom and told her that I loved her. I could hear the machines making beep noises as I watched mom's chest rise and fall. Her breathing and heart rate were slowing down by the minute. I just stood there holding her hand and watching it get slower and slower until her chest stopped moving at all and the machine made the long constant sound just like in the movies when someone passes away.

My world stopped and I felt a part of me go with her.

My legs went numb and I fell to the floor not letting go of her hand and screamed, "NO, NO, NOT HER!" I begged God to let her come back but then through all of my tears and screaming, I felt a sudden flash of calmness and through that calmness, I heard, "Mom can walk now, mom can run, climb trees, and drive any car she wants to, mom is free."

It was at that moment that I learned Gratitude.

CHAPTER ONE

Let Go Of What You Cannot Control

"For God gave us a spirit not to fear but of
power and love and self-control."
2 Timothy 1:7

*Incredible change happens in your life when you decide
to take control of what you do have power over instead of
craving control over what you don't.* ~Steve Maraboli

9:00 p.m. - The episode of *Survivor* we were watching had just ended. As I switched the TV over to the Cardinals baseball game, my wife Janet said her stomach was hurting a little bit worse. She had said something about her stomach cramping around a half hour ago. Me being more concerned with the game simply brushed it off and told her to take some Ibuprofen and maybe go lay down. Janet agreed and took some Ibuprofen, and went to bed.

9:30 p.m. - I was sitting on the couch watching the game when I heard from the hallway behind me, Janet crying and trying to say help. I got up as fast as I could and ran to the hallway to find her doubled over holding her stomach, crying and saying, "I think you need to take me to the hospital." Without questioning her, I grabbed my keys and slowly helped her out to the car. As we were walking, I asked what was hurting and if there was anything I could do to help. Through her tears, she kept saying that her stomach was hurting really bad and she didn't know what was going on.

9:35 p.m. - Once in the car, I was driving like a madman to get to the hospital. Janet was still doubled over and crying uncontrollably. All I wanted to do was make her pain go away, but I had no idea what was even wrong, and neither did she. I didn't know what to think, other than, I was happy it was later at night so there was no traffic holding me up except one car going slower than I liked. I flew by them cussing and screaming at them to get out of the way (idiots). All I could do is listen as she was in pain and I had no answers for her. The speed limit on Highway K is 45 mph until you get to a certain spot, then it switches to 50 mph. The normal 12-to-15-minute drive took us around five minutes and because I never break the law, I will just say I think it was because the traffic lights were all green.

9:40 p.m. - I pulled up to the Emergency Room door at the hospital, got out of the car, and ran as fast as I could up to the woman working behind the desk. I told her my wife was in the car, in extreme pain, and I needed a doctor right away, and I wasn't waiting in the waiting room to see anyone. She must have seen the urgency in my face because she was up and out the door with a wheelchair in seconds. Helping Janet into the chair was so painful to watch. Every movement sent her into more pain and there was nothing I could do but watch.

Wheeling her into the hospital the lady was screaming for the doctors and nurses to come help quick. By the time we got to her room, we had three doctors and four or five nurses trying to help. It pretty much took all of them to help get her into the bed. Like I said, every movement sent her into extreme pain.

Once in the bed one nurse was putting an IV in Janet's arm while one was asking me questions on what had happened. Another nurse was trying to help Janet get comfortable with pillows and blankets. Over the chaos, I could hear a doctor ordering some kind of pain medicine to help her as fast as possible.

To this day, I couldn't tell you one question that nurse asked me. I was just looking at Janet and wishing I could do anything to help her pain go away. I would look at the doctor and was waiting on him to say that he knew exactly what was wrong and how to fix her as fast as possible, but that wasn't happening. I was getting more anxious and I wanted answers right then.

The nurse with the pain medicine came flying in the room and handed the medicine to the nurse that had just finished putting in the IV. Within seconds, the medicine kicked in and Janet went limp and was asleep in just a minute or so.

This was just the first ten minutes at the hospital. My car was still out by the door still running.

9:50 p.m. - The head nurse asked if I could go move the car so it wasn't blocking the Emergency Entrance. I told her I would only if she would stay with Janet and hold her hand, I didn't want her to be alone. Even though there were six or seven people in the room.

Once outside and in the car, it was like my mind finally caught up with all the craziness, and all I could think of was the worst outcomes. What happens if she dies, or goes into a coma, or has some crazy disease where she will always be in pain, or who the hell knows what else.

I was shaking, sweating, felt cold and hot all at the same time, and my mind was a super computer on overdrive going through everything in the world.

With the car parked I opened the door ready to run back into the hospital and it hit me. The kids were home alone and when I left, they were sleeping. Now even more panic set in because I had no way to get a hold of them and no one to watch them. Running back into the hospital and back into Janet's room I seen the nurse still holding Janet's hand so I ran up to her and told her I didn't know what to do because our kids were home alone in bed sleeping. She stood up still holding Janet's hand, pulled me close to her and gave me a hug. Then as I pulled back, she wiped my cheek and told me to go to the bathroom and wash off the tears then go home and do whatever I needed to with the kids and she would stay with Janet while I was gone. I didn't even realize I was crying.

10:10 p.m. - Back at home, I found the kids were still all asleep and had no idea what was going on outside of their dream world. I found my cellphone and called a local friend to see if they could come stay with the kids while I went back to the hospital to be with Janet. They of course said yes and they were headed my way.

I sat down in my recliner to catch my breath and my brain started going a thousand miles an hour again. This time it was more about raising the kids all by myself and telling them stories of how great their mom was and I was sorry she was gone so soon. Going to graduations and weddings by myself. Seeing the grandkids and explaining how much they would have loved their grandma and how much she would have loved them.

I was thinking about how much I would miss Janet's smile and making her laugh at the stupidest things I could think to do. I missed her so much and she wasn't even gone.

The brain is a magical, amazing, and sometimes evil organ.

10:25 p.m. – My friend showed up to watch the kids. I explained what I knew was going on while smoking a cigarette, then grabbed the cellphone, keys, and wallet to head back to the hospital.

Walking back into the hospital, the nurse who was holding Janet's hand was waiting for me at the desk. She stood up and told me they took Janet back to run some tests but that she was still asleep and probably wouldn't wake up even while the tests were being done. So, I went to her at the Emergency Room and waited.

11:30 p.m. - Finally, after what seemed like hours in the room, comes two nurses followed by Janet's bed being pushed by another gentleman. Janet was still sound asleep. I stood up after they got all the machines hooked back up to her and asked one of the nurses what was going on and what they had found out. She, unfortunately, had no answers for me. She had been working in the Emergency Room the whole time and wasn't on Janet's case.

I went to Janet's side and grabbed her hand to hold. She moaned a little bit and made some other grumbling noises which might have made others think she was uncomfortable but those noises made me smile because I knew those noises, from any time I would touch her while she was sleeping. All I could see, at that point, was the Janet that I was so in love with.

11:50 p.m. - In came two doctors, with scans, pictures, and a chart of some kind. They put the pictures up on a lighted screen hanging on the wall, then asked me to come and have a look.

Once beside them, they started talking and pointing and saying *doctor words* and body parts but I had no idea what they were saying or pointing at. I finally spoke up and told them, I had no idea what was going on and please I won't be offended if they talk to me like I was a child.

One of the doctors then pointed at the screen and said that this part was supposed to be over here and that part was supposed to be over there and he kept pointing and saying that nothing was in its right place and they DIDN'T know why.

There was pressure being put on one of her lungs and on her heart. Those were the two biggest things I understood.

The two doctors left the room and within a minute another different doctor comes in, looks at the pictures, grabs the chart and looks through it for a minute then looks over at me and says, "We're doing all we can and your wife is stable right now," then leaves as fast as he came in.

3:00 a.m. - For three hours, I sat there holding Janet's hand watching nurses and doctors come in and out. Checking her vitals and the machines, and every once in a while, someone would ask if I was okay. I wanted to scream at them and tell them I'm not okay because my wife is laying in this bed and no one is giving us answers. But I didn't because I was pretty sure they didn't even know what was going on. I was just happy because Janet was asleep through this whole time, and while I knew she was in pain, I'm sure it would have been a lot worse if she would have been awake.

3:15 a.m. - One of the doctors came in the room and told me that they had emailed Janet's scans over to another doctor at another hospital and were waiting for a response. He then explained that he had never seen anything like this before and as a matter of fact, none of the doctors in the ER had ever seen anything like it. All he could tell me was her inside parts weren't where they were supposed to be.

As he was finishing up another doctor and three nurses came flying in the room saying they had to get her prepped and ready for surgery. The doctor they had emailed was on his way in and said that she needed to be ready by the time he got there.

3:35 a.m. - In walks this little bitty old man with a foreign accent that I could barely understand. He got everyone lined out on what to do then turned to me and asked if I was the husband. I answered, "Yes," and asked back to him, "What is going on?" His response was simple but devastating, "Kiss your wife and tell her you love her then when were gone, look up what a Volvulus is, we should be in surgery for around three hours." Then he was gone. As soon as they were out of sight, I was on my phone looking up Volvulus.

Volvulus definition: An obstruction due to twisting or knotting of the gastrointestinal tract.

In Sammy terms which is much easier: Her intestines weren't connected to her body anymore that's why everything looked like it was in the wrong place.

I spent the next hour calling her parents, friends, coworkers, and boss just to let them know what little bit I knew. I'm sure they felt like me, lost, confused, frustrated, and sad. I just sat in the waiting room watching TV and waiting for someone to come get me and tell me she was okay.

At around the three-and-a-half-hour mark I started to get really worried because no one had told me anything. I called the nurses' station but they didn't have an update. Then around the five-hour mark, I started to get nervous and a little pissed.

I, again, called the nurses' station and the nurse told me she would personally go find out what was going on. Thirty minutes later, she came out to the waiting room and told me that it was a little more than just the volvulus that they were dealing with but she was doing okay.

11:45 a.m. - After almost nine hours, the little doctor came walking into the waiting room telling me Janet was in recovery and doing fine. Then he started explaining what happened.

When we are born, our intestine connects itself to our body, kind of like glues itself to our sides. This process happens in the first few weeks after birth. For one in a million people after birth this process doesn't take place. It usually affects around 12 inches of the intestine, causing major stomach pain and has to be operated on and cut out. In Janet's case the doctor said almost 26 inches were not connected and it had moved around to the front of her body putting pressure on her heart, almost collapsing her lungs, and harming every other organ. He said she was not a one in a million she was more like one in 100 million. He also said that if she would have tried to tough it out till morning she would have passed away.

After weeks of recovery, I am happy to say Janet is doing great and being her rotten self again. I Love You, Dear.

I told this whole story just so I could tell everyone of you reading this, a message.

You control almost nothing that happens outside of your body and it is up to you, in most cases, how much or how little you control inside your body.

What and how much control did I have that night?

I controlled the car driving Janet to the hospital. I controlled my emotions, words, actions, and reactions. That's it. I was not in control of Janet's health or wellbeing. I was not in control of anything that took place at that hospital.

What and how much control did Janet have that night?

She let me know her stomach was hurting and she needed to go to the hospital. After that, she had no more control over anything. A person laying in a hospital bed in major pain and could possibly die had no control over the outcome of that night.

Who had control of that night?

- The electric company for the electricity of the machines and the lights.
- The water company for water for her surgery.
- The technicians for doing the tests.
- The nurses for doing more than I can list.
- The doctors for understanding and accepting they didn't have the knowledge to help this woman. They also did a lot more than I can list.
- And the little doctor for having the knowledge to help Janet and save her life.

You can do this timeline test on any event that has happened in your own life to try and figure out what you were truly in control of and what you were not. I think it might surprise you how much you had no control over but yet you hold yourself to blame.

I could have blamed myself for so much from that night. Why was I watching the game instead of watching Janet? Why didn't I drive faster to the hospital? Why didn't I force the doctors to give me answers faster? Why, why, why?

BECAUSE I DIDN'T HAVE CONTROL.

One of the questions I get most often is, "How do I find happiness, love, and joy? How do I find Gratitude?"

You have to look for it, feel it, and embrace it.

If I asked you to write down everything I was grateful for that night, I would bet that your list would mainly be the big stuff.

The doctors and nurses.

The machines that did the scans.

The car to get to the hospital. And maybe a couple more.

My list would go like this:

- I'm happy for gas in the car.
- I'm grateful we had clothes.
- I love that my friend who came over to watch my kids.
- I'm grateful for the car running, and getting us where we needed to go.
- I'm grateful my arms, legs, and eyes were working properly.
- I'm happy Janet didn't try and tough it out and came to me in pain.
- I'm happy we lived so close to the hospital.
- I could keep going but I think you get the point and we haven't even left the driveway.

Anytime you find yourself in a bad situation, angry, stressed, or when anxiety is about to kick in take five deep breaths and ask yourself this question, **"What do I control right now, in my life?"**

CHAPTER TWO

Drama and Negativity

"Consider it pure joy, my brothers and sisters,
whenever you face trials of many kinds.
Because you know that the testing of your faith produces perseverance."
James 1: 2-3

Five Traits of Negative People

1. They get jealous of others easily.
2. They believe they are better or more important than others.
3. They blame everything on everyone else but themselves.
4. They point out everyone else's faults.
5. They only see the bad in every situation.

I can honestly say I have been every one of these people at multiple times in my life. Can you be honest and say the same?

Living in a life of gratitude, I now look at this list in a totally different mindset. When I see people who are being one of the things on the list, I'd ask myself, "How can I help them? What are they missing or wanting in their life? What are they going through right now?" In other words, I empathize with them instead of outright judging them.

Three Stories – Food For Thought

Puppies For Sale

An old farmer was at the end of his driveway, nailing a sign up on a post that said, "Four Puppies for Sale." As he was tacking the last nail, he felt a tug at his pants. He turned around to see a little boy standing there. The little boy looked up at the old farmer and said "I would like to buy one of the puppies." The farmer told the little boy, "These puppies are a rare breed and are very expensive." The little boy told the old farmer that all he had was thirty-five cents and wanted to know if that would be enough money to at least look at the puppies. The old farmer told the boy to keep his money but he could still come look at the puppies.

When they got over to the pen with the dog house, four little puppies came running out. They were barking, jumping, and full of energy. Then the little boy seen a fifth puppy come from the house. This puppy couldn't run because it was born with a bad leg. Even with its bad leg he still barked and seemed very happy.

The little boy looked at the old farmer and said, "How much is that puppy? That's the one I would like to buy?" The farmer told the little boy, "That puppy is lame and wouldn't be able to run and play with you."

The little boy lifted up his pant leg showing the farmer his prosthetic leg and said, "I don't think I will be doing a lot of running, so we should be a perfect match."

The farmer reached down with tears in his eyes and grabbed the puppy then handed him to the little boy and said, "Here yah go, this one is free."

The little boy grabbed the puppy with so much delight then grabbed the thirty-five cents from his pocket and handed it to the farmer then said, "This puppy is worth all the money I have."

The Rich Drywaller

When I first started doing drywall, there was a drywall hanger that we would talk about because of his clothing and car and just how poor he was. He was a man in his fifties that still wore clothes he had in high school. He said that new clothes were too expensive and as long as the clothes he had fit then what's the use in buying new ones. He had never bought a vehicle in his life he always got the cars of his family that had passed away. He would do the upkeep on those vehicles and drive them till the tires fell off. Never was married or had kids, he lived in a little crappy trailer that looked like it would fall apart at any moment.

Working as a union drywall hanger and doing side jobs all the time, we never understood why he was so broke, and lived so poor. He easily made over $100,000 a year.

When he passed away the state had to sell off what little stuff he had and move the trailer to a dump to get rid of it. When they moved the trailer, they found hundreds of holes with cans and jars in them. Totaling over a million dollars in those cans and jars plus a certified letter that said he wanted all the money to go to a local church. When the church was asked what affiliation, this guy had with them the preacher answered, "We have never even heard his name before and are pretty sure he has never been to one of our services."

All we ever did was talk behind his back and tease him about how his life sucked so bad. The reality was he lived the life he wanted and his wealth came not from what possessions he had in this world but from what he gave back when he was gone.

The Upset River

At the end of another beautiful day, the river began to complain again. Every day at sundown the river would complain, "I'm so tired of moving all day and night, it's not fair that everything else gets to go to sleep and rest and I always have to keep moving. It's not fair and I wish I could just stop moving and dry up."

Finally, after months of listening to the river complain the mountain next to where the river ran said in a roaring voice, "Will you please shut up and quit complaining?" The mountain then explained that sitting around resting every day wasn't exactly the dream life either, but being able to sit and rest allowed him to see all the beauty around him.

He got to see the animals being born and grow into adults. He watched the seasons change the trees and plants into different colors and regrow their leaves every year. He also got to admire the beautiful river that ran in his valley.

The river that gave life to all of those animals, trees, and plants. The river that could withstand all the seasons mother nature would put it through. The river that the mountain would sit and watch day after day moving without a care in the world.

Mountain: "Now, do you understand just how powerful and mighty you really are river? Now, do you see that you bring life, happiness, and joy to everyone in your presence? Now, do know how much we all really love you? So please don't ever stop moving."

River: "I never thought of myself in these many ways. Thank you, mountain, for being a part of my life and I promise this, I will never complain again and I will never stop moving."

When I decided to write this chapter, I could only think about the negative people in my life or the ones I have encountered throughout my life. The ones who never held themselves accountable. The ones who always seemed to be mad at everyone else. I could go on and on naming all the different kinds of negative people but instead I got to thinking about this book and how it is supposed to be a guide for you to live a life of gratitude, not a book about how other people suck. The easy answer is just to avoid them. If they are family members or close friends learn to love them from a distance. Maybe, they're coworkers and you have no choice but to try and find good in them (or smack them in the head every once in a while, which is really what we all want to do).

I told these three stories as a reflection of my own pitfalls of living a life of gratitude, and I'm pretty sure something in these stories resonated with you.

How many of us got upset with the farmer for putting no value at all on the puppy with a bad leg?

How many of us have judged someone by their appearance or belongings before we ever got to know them?

How many of us do not see the value we bring to this beautiful world every day?

Unfortunately, what we see and think we know is how we judge our world and that is why we feel so much negativity around us. We take the actions of people and make assumptions-based on absolutely nothing. We find faults in others fortunes just so we may feel better about our own lives.

To live a life of gratitude is finding value in all things in this world. (Good or Bad, Happiness or Sadness, yes, even Negativity or Positivity). This includes in yourself.

What would your life look like with no judgement, jealousy, or blame?

How would it feel to be able to look in the mirror and see that strong powerful river that brings joy, happiness, life, and love to those around you?

Gratitude can overcome any negative person, thought, or moment in your life when you start looking for it.

Go outside and find one beautiful thing to look at. Now concentrate on it and take five deep breaths. With the last three breaths close your eyes and feel the air in your lungs, feel your body being filled, and see that beautiful thing from moments ago through your mind.

Do this exercise in moments of stress or anxiety to give your mind a positive shift. Do this exercise as many times as it takes per day and eventually you will start to feel the power of Gratitude.

CHAPTER THREE

Negative Self Talk

"I can do all this through Him who gives me strength."
Philippians 4:12

CAN'T is a word used by individuals that never want to try, have given up before they started, tell themselves they are worthless, and want the world to bow down to them and their low expectations of life.

THAT'S NOT YOU.

Somewhere in our past, we started to believe we weren't enough. We stopped talking about our dreams and aspirations and started listening to that crazy voice in our head. For most of us, it only took a single moment or one unfortunate event to convince us that we just don't have what it takes. From that one time, we had another one, then another one, and another, until we forgot what it was to win. We lost control of our most valuable asset in life. Ourselves.

A life of Gratitude has a lot to do with what we tell ourselves. The truth is that there is only one person who has heard every thought and word that has ever come from your mind. Well, I'm here to tell you that it's time to talk back and start controlling that voice in your head.

A man is walking around the circus grounds when he sees three enormous elephants in one of the tents. As he is looking at the amazing creatures, he notices each one of them has a small rope tied around its neck that is connected to a small pole stuck in the ground. The man doesn't understand how these massive giants are not pulling the poles out of the ground and just running away.

He finds one of the trainers and asked him, "How is it possible that the elephants are not pulling the posts out of the ground and running away?"

The trainer tells the man, "When they are babies, we use the same rope and pole to tie them up to, at that age and size they are unable to pull the pole out of the ground and over the years they train themselves to believe they can never pull the pole out of the ground." The man walked away in disbelief that these great powerful creatures would train themselves to believe they are so weak and helpless.

You are that Great Powerful Creature. Time to pull the pole out of the ground.

Unfortunately, this story hits to close to home for so many of us. When we are born, we don't know the word can't and we have no limiting beliefs about ourselves. We are not weak and helpless; we are strong and smart. The world is simply our playground.

Some time in our baby years everything changes. Initially, we get told we can do things, such as crawl, stand up, walk, and evolve in every way. When we do these things, we even get praised and celebrated.

Then something switches or happens and we get introduced to Can't. Before you know it, all the things you were being praised for doing become your downfall. Can't touch this. Can't touch that. Can't go in that room. Can't climb up that. Can't, Can't, Can't.

Being a father of three and now having three grandchildren, I totally understand how we introduce *Can't* into our children's lives so fast. Mainly because it's our stuff they want to touch, carry around, and possibly break. Also, as parents we look out for our kids' safety. I'm not saying we're bad parents or we're the reason our kids don't follow their dreams, but in a roundabout upside-down kind of way we are. Not the bad parent part but more focused on the *not following your dreams* part.

We introduced them into a world of limiting beliefs, fears, and unfulfilled dreams.

The reality is we teach them these lessons through our actions and beliefs. We tell kids that they can be anything they want when they grow up but then they watch us not go after our dreams or achieve the things that we said we wanted in our own lives.

From high up in the tree top, Amanda could see for miles and miles. She could see the Vaughn farm which was around eight miles away. Turning to her left, she could see town and some cars driving past the interstate. Way up in this tree, she felt the wind on her arms causing goose bumps, along with the smell of freshness that you could only get from being this close to the clouds. She dreamt of someday seeing the stars from a rocket ship and the feeling of weightlessness, of being in space.

Coming out of the space dream amongst the stars, she could hear her dad screaming from the ground for her to get out of that damn tree before she falls and breaks her arm, or, even worse gets killed.

As she climbs down, she feels the anxiety of knowing she was in trouble. Her dad had told her before to stay out of the tree. She fears the punishment she knows she is getting and anticipating to happen. What was waiting for her at the bottom of the tree was unknown and that feeling caused her to start crying.

When her feet hit the ground, her dad was right there grabbing her arm and saying, "Quit that damn crying, I told you not to climb that tree anymore and now you're getting a spanking."

Through the fear of a broken arm or death and the pain from the spanking, Amanda never climbed that tree again. She never went to space and she had a major fear of heights after that day. This story took place when she was eight years old.

The moral to this story is that most of our life long habits and fears are developed in moments just like this. The dad had no idea he had just imprinted an emotional trauma on his daughter. He had no idea he had just changed the trajectory of his daughter's life. He had no idea he had just shattered her dreams. Crazy part is that he was actually trying to keep her safe.

It's always easier to look back on our past and say "I wish I would have or I could have, but." It's painful, sad, and depressing to think that at one time you could have done anything. It's even more painful to believe and tell yourself that you still can't right now. I'm here today to tell you that *Can't* is no longer an option.

I'm forty-eight years old, five foot six, and a thick two hundred pounds, and I Can slam a basketball. I got D's and F's in writing and English classes all through school and never thought I could write a book, but I am and I Can. I never went to college or knew anything about owning a business, but I have had a successful painting company for twelve years. Because I CAN.

A group of frogs were traveling through the woods when two of the frogs fell into a deep well. The other frogs gathered around the opening of the well and started screaming that the well was too deep and they should just give up.

The two frogs in the well ignored the screams and started jumping as hard as they could, but after a few jumps the one frog decided they were probably right and jumped the rest of the way down the well to his death.

After seeing this, the last frog in the well looked up and seen the other frogs still screaming for him to give up and jump to his death, too. With all his might he jumped harder and harder until he finally made it out. Once he was out the other frogs asked him why he didn't just jump to his death also?

He simply replied, "With you guys rooting for me, I believed I could get out." They later found out he was deaf and couldn't hear any of their negative comments.

When you start using the word Can you stop hearing and believing all the Can't comments.

> Me: "I really need to start working out and eating better so I can start feeling better."
> Brain: "We can't start today; Starbucks has a sale and our favorite show is on tonight."
> Me: "We can skip Starbucks and go for a walk before the show tonight."
> Brain: "How about if we get Starbucks, watch our show, and promise that we will start first thing next Monday?"

Me: "Okay, but only if we promise."
Brain: "Deal."

Easiest negotiation in the world is a lie to yourself. You want to know why? Because no one else heard the lie to talk back to it or hold you accountable.

You have to learn to talk back, not accept defeat, and be determined to get your way. When the fighting in my head is more than I can handle I physically talk to my brain.

With physically talking, I have more weapons than just arguing with myself in my head. I can hear the words, feel the words, and change the tone of my voice to be more demanding.

When I first started this self-development journey, I decided I wanted to start getting up at 4 a.m. I usually got up at 5:30 or 6 a.m. anyway, so this should be an easy transition.

Nope. I fought and fought with myself, every day to get up, and most days it still wasn't at 4 a.m. Finally, one night, I sat on my bed and started talking,

Me: "I am getting up at 4 a.m."
Brain: "Nope."
Me: "Why not?"
Brain: "It's too early. DUH."
Brain: "How about 4:30 a.m.?"
Me: "No, I want 4 a.m."
Brain: "How about 4:15 a.m.?"
Me: "No, but how about 4:05 a.m.?"
Brain: "4:10 a.m. is the best I can do."
Me: "Deal, see you at 4:10 a.m., my friend."

While I made this argument sound fast and easy, I will let you know I had this argument for weeks and weeks. Fighting with your brain is no different than any other fight. If you really want to win the fight then you never give up, no matter how long it takes. That happened around five years ago and I still get up every day at 4:10 a.m.

The power of words is very underrated in our world. As I said earlier in this chapter, we are the only person that has ever heard every word that has come out of our mouths. That means we have heard from our own voice that I can't, I don't want, I won't, not today, it's not for me, I'm not able, I'm not worthy. We have heard all of these negative things plus so many more, not from other people but from ourselves.

My question to you is this, "Would you allow anyone else on this planet to put you down this much? Would you allow someone else to tell you that "you can't", or would you do the opposite and show them that you can?"

A life of Gratitude is something you Can have, Do deserve, Is for you, and You are more than worthy of having.

Start saying that to yourself every day until you believe it, then believe you Can have it every day.

That's a Life of Unstoppable Gratitude.

CHAPTER FOUR

Evaluate Your Environment

"For where your treasure is, there your heart will be also."
Mattew 6:21

If you can see it, hear it, touch it, or, even smell it, I would consider whatever IT is, to be part of your environment. If IT affects your mood, feelings, or mindset then IT is definitely environmental.

While I could write an entire book on this subject (and a lot of books have been written on this subject), I would like to cover what I consider the main two environments we deal with every day.

Who do you surround yourself with?
What do you surround yourself with?

I watched a video the other day about a duck that acted like a chicken. The duck was placed in the chicken coop so he wouldn't run away. The owner explained that within just a few months the duck started acting like the chickens even to the point that he would make noises like the roosters.

Next thing I know, I've watched twenty plus videos about animals acting like other animals. I saw turkeys acting like ducks, sheep acting like dogs, roosters acting like penguins, and even a rhino acting like a goat.

So, the next time you hear someone say, "If it walks like a duck, swims like a duck, and quacks like a duck, it must be a duck," you can politely say, "Don't be so sure of that, it just might be a chicken."

Watching all those videos, I realized one thing. Jim Rohn was correct when he said, "You are the average of the five people you spend most of your time with."

This realization got me thinking about my past and how many transformations I have been through in my life.

When I was in the Army I hung out with certain soldiers, mainly the ones who liked to power lift and do steroids. With these people, I got physically strong as hell, but also very angry all of the time.

After the Army I did Martial Arts for a few years, my crew then consisted of other martial artists. Mainly people that wanted to do Mixed Martial Arts and cage fights like the UFC.

From there I started doing drywall. Construction guys were my people and I loved it. We were all about making money doing side jobs. That was pretty much all we talked about. Money, Money, Money.

After the 2008 shit show of an economy and having the worst financial year ever in my life, I decided I would open my own company. I spent around five years mainly working by myself and barely getting by. What I learned is: I was great at drywall and painting, but had no clue how to run a business. Finally, after a couple more years of minimal growth and being broke, I was introduced to networking, marketing, and everything else it really took to own and run a business.

Fellow business owners and networkers were now my tribe. I felt like I had finally found my people. Like-minded people that just wanted to succeed in business and help other people be successful in their businesses.

Throughout those years, I had many other adventures and many other tribes of people along the way, but one thing became very clear, I ALWAYS BECOME LIKE THE PEOPLE I HUNG AROUND WITH THE MOST, and a sometimes that wasn't a good thing.

The worst one of all was when and how I started smoking cigarettes. I remember walking over to the car that the smokers all hung out at before school and asking one of the guys if I could get a smoke from him. After giving me one, he asked why I was trying to hang out with them since I played football and was a jock? I will never forget my answer that day, "Because you guys are way cooler."

While I have made a lot of friends over the years by being a smoker, I can also say that walking over to that car that day is one of the biggest regrets I have in my life.

I hear a lot of people refer to these times as seasons of our lives.

I would like you to read Jim Rohn's quote one more time, "You are the average of the five people you spend most of your time with."

I reference this quote when I talk about cutting people out of your life or loving someone from a distance, and I almost always get push back on it. I have found that the people that push back have one of these things in common. Understanding that not everyone wants to move forward with you in your life. AND THAT'S OKAY. Not everyone wants to travel down the same road as you, some people are happy with where they are, some people we grow apart from, some people will even get mad at you for leaving them behind. AND THAT'S OK.

The right people will always be there, they just might be at a distance. I still have friends I keep up from the Army, Martial Arts, and construction. When we do talk, we don't talk about business, growth, self-development, or, the ins and outs of writing a book. We talk about family, holidays, and past memories. None of these people are in my immediate five but I still care for every one of them.

Think of it like this, if I want to learn how to ride a horse and be a cowboy am I going to hang around car mechanics that don't have horses? Maybe I want to be a police officer, so hanging around my pothead friends who play Xbox all day, wouldn't be a good choice.

Living a life of Gratitude would be so much harder, if not impossible, around a bunch negative, my life sucks, the world is against me, type of people. These negative people can and will include your friends and family. You have to learn to LOVE THEM FROM A DISTANCE.

In March 2020, the world as we knew it, took on a drastic change. Overnight, our lives were turned upside down and inside out. Most of the places that we would be called regulars, closed down: coffee shops, gyms, stores, churches, and so much more. Our environment changed so fast; we didn't know how to react. So, we did what we would normally do, FREAKED OUT.

We made sure we filled up our vehicles and extra cans with gas (that most of us wouldn't drive for months). We cleaned out the stores of food and supplies (aka toilet paper crisis of 2020). We overwhelmed the hospitals (sometimes because of a simple cough or sneeze). We did all of these things, mainly because, we felt like we lost control over our own choices in life.

We are habit driven creatures, first and foremost. When we couldn't get our coffee or breakfast sandwich like we did every other day for the last however many years, our brains automatically go into defense mode. It was trying to protect us from change, because nothing is scarier than change.

I will let you in on a little secret to living a life of gratitude. You have to be willing to change! Change your feelings, attitude, and surroundings.

Let me start by saying, I'm not a licensed therapist or psychologist. I use the knowledge I have trained and studied in mindset, body language, and energy to give advice. I will always recommend seeing a licensed professional. That being said, a lot of people contact me for advice, especially in mindset.

A friend of mine called me and said they were having a lot of anxiety around certain things in their lives and didn't know how to deal with them. Anxiety that would cause uncontrollable crying, body weakness, and nightmarish mind shifts. My simple, but not easy advice, was to start by changing their environment every time the anxiety would start to show up.

Changing their environment meant a change in scenery. In other words, if they were in their kitchen then go into another room of the house. If they were in their office at work, then go to another office or even the restroom. The one I recommend the most is to go outside, if at all possible. If you are already outside then move to a different area outside.

I believe in energy, both positive and negative. So, when I recommend moving to different areas, it's mainly to remove yourself from the energy that currently surrounds you. Energy is found in everything in and around us. If I'm in my office at home and I start feeling any type of negativity, I remove myself from my desk, chair, bookshelves, floor, and the room.

Once my friend had changed environments (preferably outside), I recommended finding one thing to focus on and find peace, beauty, and gratitude in it. Look at it like you never have before. See the beautiful color of the grass, imagine it running through your toes with bare feet. Imagine the smell of cut grass going through your nose and down to your lungs, filling your body with calmness.

Last, but not least, it's to control your breathing. I recommend five deep four second breaths. Four seconds in and four seconds out. The first two breaths concentrate on the breathing and time limit. The last three breaths, close your eyes and feel the air coming into your body, feel it moving throughout your blood and touching every pore of skin.

Shifting Your Mindset Through Your Environment: RECAP

1. Move to a different area or space.
2. Concentrate on one item.
3. Control your breathing.

The reason I recommend all three of these movements is because they build on top of each other. The brain doesn't think in the positive and negative at the same time. Build on the positives and eliminate the negatives.

Let me make this very clear. This is NOT a one-time-and-done technique. This is something done over and over, many times a day (especially when starting to use it.) It is a practiced technique that you will get better and stronger at, over time. Until it becomes a habit.

Back to my friend and how this has helped them.

Friend: "I'm kind of freaked out right now."
Me: "Why?"
Friend: "I felt my anxiety building up and kind of blacked out and woke up outside staring at a tree."
Me: "Do you remember walking outside now?"
Friend: "Yes, I remember everything now, I just don't understand how, I just did it without thinking about it."
Me: "Have you ever been driving in your car to a destination you normally go to and when you get there you can't remember parts of the drive there? Is there anything else you do normally and naturally every day that you don't have to think about yet you just do it? Walking, talking, eating, and so on?"
Friend: "Well, yeah, duh. But those are just normal things that I do."
Me: "Is your anxiety gone?"
Friend: "Yes, and it didn't last very long or get as bad."
Me: "Welcome to the wonderful world of new habits and controlling more of your unconscious mind."
Friend: "Wow, that's really cool."

To end this chapter the most I can say is this, "A life of gratitude does not only come from inside yourself but also from that which you allow around yourself."

CHAPTER FIVE

Gratitude and Honesty

*"In everything give thanks: for this is the will of
God in Christ Jesus concerning you."*
1 Thessalonians 5:18

There is only one person on this entire planet that has heard every word come out of your mouth, every thought that has went through your head, every lie you have ever told, and every negative feeling or emotion that flows through your body. YOU!

One day while at Home Depot, an employee and I were buying some separate items for a job we were about to start. When we were done at checkout, we proceeded to the truck to head to the jobsite. Once in the truck, my employee looked at me and said, "Hold on a minute, I have to run back inside."

After just a few minutes, he returned and everything seemed okay. I asked him if he forgot something or just needed something else. He replied that he had somehow missed paying for an item so he had to go back in and pay for it.

The item he was talking about wasn't anything big or expensive, it was a two-dollar item. In my mind I couldn't believe that he had just wasted his time going back in and paying for it. I knew that if it would have been me, I wouldn't have gone back in and paid for it.

I asked him why he was so concerned with paying for such a cheap item, especially from a big box store that wouldn't even realize or care that it was gone?

His answer would change my life.

He said just because the big box store may not realize it or care, he knew what he had done and did care. He cared so much not for the big box store but for the place that made the item, the trucker who shipped it, the person that stocked it, and the person that sold it to him. That silly, cheap item made sure a lot of people got paid and fed their families.

This one-time employee became my friend, then my best friend, and until my last breath my brother. Love yah, Norm.

To have that kind of honesty and integrity is exactly what this whole book has been about. To be so grateful for complete strangers and their families, along with knowing your own values and not exceeding the boundaries you have set for yourself. That's a life of joy, love, and gratitude.

That kind of life only comes by doing the hardest thing you will ever have to do in your life. Hold yourself accountable.

There is a program called 75 hard. (I would recommend everyone doing it). It is five must be done daily challenges, for 75 days straight. NO DAYS OFF.

1. Two forty-five-minute workouts done at least three hours apart. One has to be done outside in the elements. (Sun, rain, snow, wind.)
2. Read ten pages of a self-help type of book. Not an e-book, an actual book you hold and physically read.
3. Drink 1 gallon of water.
4. Follow a diet or meal plan. Any one of the thousands that are out there, just pick one. Also, NO alcohol.
5. Take a full body selfie. Every day.

The first time I attempted 75 hard, I failed on day 59. We had went camping for the weekend and I went to bed Friday night thinking I had completed all 5 tasks for the day, then Saturday morning

I woke up to see a notification on my phone that I had forgotten to take my daily picture.

That day, I had two choices. One, I take the picture and log it onto the 75 hard app and act like nothing happened. Two, I would be honest with myself that I had failed to complete all the tasks from the day prior and I hold myself accountable.

The mental toughness that is developed during 75 hard only happens through holding yourself accountable. Every day on every task.

I proceeded to have a great weekend with family and friends, explaining to all of them how I had forgotten the picture and I would restart from day one, Monday morning. I did restart Monday morning and I did complete the 75 hard program, 75 days later.

The only way to live a complete life of gratitude is through honesty, integrity, and accountability with yourself. The last four chapters have been about the three-character traits that we should all want to live our lives by.

Understand and realize what you do control in your own life, along with being truthful with yourself about your past and what you have no control over. Once you loosen the grip and eventually let go of that thing, moment, or situation from your past, you will start noticing what you do control becomes stronger. What you figure out is, that which you thought you controlled was actually controlling you. Your power and gratitude come from letting go.

Do a self-check on ALL of the people you have in your life. I recommend using a bullseye target chart.

1. Use yourself as the bullseye.
2. Then, start writing names of individuals who are In the circle directly closest to you. These would possibly be your wife, husband, kids, mom, and dad. People in your household, that no matter what, you see them every day.
3. Next circle would be really good friends or people you work with. These people you might see every day but possibly not by choice.

4.   Next circle would be the next layer of people in your life. Maybe this circle would be people you see four or five times a week.

5.   From there you keep making circles as far out as the relationships go.

NOW comes the honesty part. In each circle are those individuals helping you achieve a life of gratitude or holding you from it? Do some of these people need to be moved back to a different circle?

Hold yourself accountable to the truth. Sometimes the truth is that we have to love people from a distance, even the ones we love the most. Can you say I'm grateful to have that person in my life because they bring me peace of mind and body? Do you feel a certain joy and happiness when in their presence?

Start healthy self-talk. I recommend making a chart and write down some of the statements that you find yourself saying over and over.

Negative Self-Talk	Positive Reframe
I'm so dumb.	Whoops, I made a mistake.
Nobody likes me.	I like me.
I give up, I just suck.	This is hard but I will keep going.
I never get anything right.	I haven't figured it out yet.
I'm not good enough.	I am great.

If you are honest with doing this chart and start practicing *Positive Reframes*, you will start to build new positive habits and develop new positive mindsets. Eliminate the words Can't and Try. There is absolutely nothing you Can't do, and quit telling yourself "Your trying," (you either doing or you're not.) Trying is a state of mind so you don't have to hold yourself fully accountable. Words will help you achieve the greatness and happiness you deserve.

Look around yourself right now.

- What do you see?
- Who is around you?
- How do these things and people make you feel?
- Is there anything you could change that would make you happier?
- Is there anyone that maybe you need to start spending a little less time with?
- Is there anyone who you need to cut off completely?
- What boundaries and standards have you set for yourself and those around you?

These are seven questions you should be asking yourself all of the time. If answered honestly then your environment will be set up for your success.

The last few paragraphs are based on honesty, integrity, and accountability. Go back through them and do the exercises. These are some of the hardest tasks you will ever have to do, because you have to hold yourself accountable to be honest with yourself. I will promise you this "Living a life of Gratitude is totally worth it."

In closing of this book, I truly hope you took away some lessons to start implementing, a new appreciation of what gratitude is and how powerful it can be in your life, and a mindset of knowing gratitude is in every one of us.

Gratitude is a gift.

You are a gift.

GRATITUDE = YOU

CPSIA information can be obtained
at www.ICGtesting.com
Printed in the USA
LVHW041413170523
747241LV00004B/163